Snowdonia

SNOWDONIA
W. A. Poucher

Constable London

First published in Great Britain 1990
by Constable and Company Limited
10 Orange Street London WC2H 7EG
Copyright © 1990 pictures, the Estate of W. A. Poucher
Copyright © 1990 text, John Poucher
ISBN 0 09 469620 9
Text filmset by BAS Printers Ltd, Hampshire
Printed and bound in Spain by
Graficas Estella, S. A.

The photographs

Preface

As only one book of my late father's colour
photographs of this beautiful country – *Wales*
(1981) – has so far appeared in print, I decided to
examine the stock of his Welsh transparencies in
my possession to determine if it was possible to
select a further hundred pictures to form a second
volume. I hope you will agree with me that this
exercise, whose result is seen in the following
pages, was rewarding.

Over a period of many years, the exploration
of the Welsh countryside, and particularly of the
mountainous area around Snowdon, gave my
father much pleasure, and I well remember my
first visit there with him when I was ten years old.
One of my memories is of our ascent of Snowdon
over Crib Goch, quite an undertaking for one of
such tender years. Another is of an expedition

over Glyder Fach from Pen y Gwryd, with snow
on the tops, and of descending Bristly Ridge
which was a high adventure for me at the time.

Since then, in company with my wife, I have
spent many happy hours tramping over the hills
and through the forests of this delightful part of
Wales.

You will find that the pictures which follow are
arranged, as is the case in all the other books in
the series, roughly in sequence – in this case from
north to south – so that visitors can follow them
by car, or on foot.

John Poucher
Gate Ghyll, High Brigham
Cockermouth, Cumbria
1990

Great Orme Head

Llandudno is a popular seaside resort on the coast
of North Wales. It is set in a bay between two
headlands, Great and Little Orme: Marine Drive,
a toll road, encircles the former.

Aber Falls

These well-known falls occur where the Afon
Rhaeadr plunges some 200 feet over a cliff. Aber
lies on the A55, not far from Llanfairfechan, and
is the starting-point for walks in the northern
Carneddau.

Llyn Geirionydd

There is good sailing on this remote and peaceful
lake, which may be reached by a narrow road that
leaves the A5 at the Ugly House, or from Trefriw
on the B5106.

Llyn Crafnant

(overleaf)

This tranquil lake is in fact a reservoir on which
sailing is permitted. It lies a mile or so west of
Llyn Geirionydd, and may also be reached by
road from Trefriw, or on foot from Capel Curig.

Afon Lledr

(overleaf pp 20/21)

This delightful river threads the Lledr valley,
passing Dolwyddelan with its ruined castle,
before joining the River Conway south of
Betws-y-Coed.

Bridge at Ty-hyll

Ty-hyll or 'the ugly house' is situated beside the
A5 some 3 miles east of Capel Curig, where the
road passes over the Afon Llugwy on its way to
Betws-y-Coed. Swallow Falls lie a little further
downstream.

Colour above Capel Curig
(*overleaf*)

In this lovely autumn scene the Pinnacles of Capel Curig appear on the left, and Tryfan on the right of the picture.

Afon Llugwy

This sinuous river, rising in Ffynnon Llugwy, flows through Capel Curig where it plunges over the Cyfyng Falls. This picture was taken from Pont Cyfyng, looking upstream.

The Glyders from Clogwyn Mawr

(overleaf)

The small eminence of Clogwyn Mawr lies not far from Capel Curig and may be traversed on a walk from there to Creigiau Gleision. It provides a surprisingly good viewpoint for the Glyders and the Carneddau. Bristly Ridge is seen here over Gallt yr Ogof, with Tryfan on the right.

Llyn Cowlyd

This lake, lying cradled between Pen yr Helgi-Du and Creigiau Gleision, is a reservoir. The picture was taken from the head of the lake.

The Carneddau
in winter
(overleaf)

The southern bastions of this group of hills are seen here, from a viewpoint near Capel Curig, in snowy raiment.

The Carneddau
in autumn
(overleaf pp 34/35)

Here, with superb autumn colours and glowing bracken, a very different scene is portrayed from the one before. The viewpoint is by the Pinnacles of Capel Curig.

Ffynnon Llugwy

Set amidst the Carneddau peaks, this reservoir is
seen here from Craig yr Ysfa. A walk up the
Water Board road from the A5 makes a short but
pleasant outing.

Craig yr Ysfa

(overleaf)

This craggy ridge connects Pen yr Helgi-Du and
Carnedd Llywelyn, which appears in the
background. The ridge may easily be traversed
during the course of a walk to Carnedd Llywelyn,
and there is climbing on the Cwm Eigiau side.

Cwm Lloer

This wild cwm, seen here with its lake, Ffynnon
Lloer, from Pen yr Ole Wen, may be reached on
a walk from Llyn Ogwen by the path which
ascends along the Afon Lloer.

Carnedd Ddafydd and Elidir Fawr

Carnedd Ddafydd, brooding on the left of the
picture, is second in height in the Carneddau only
to Carnedd Llywelyn. Elidir Fawr lies in the
Glyder group on the other side of Nant Ffrancon.

Ysgolion Duon

These fine cliffs, commonly known as Black
Ladders, lie at the head of Cwm Llafar and are a
bastion of Carnedd Ddafydd. Their foot may be
reached at the end of a pleasant walk up the valley
from Bethesda.

Gallt yr Ogof

(overleaf)

This rugged hill is the first of the Glyders group to be seen when motoring westwards along the A5 from Capel Curig. Its summit may be traversed on a ridge walk from Capel Curig to Glyder Fach.

Tryfan

The most popular view of this striking and
elegant mountain is the one seen here – from the
east. Wintry conditions show its profile to
advantage.

The other side of Tryfan
(*overleaf*)

Here, with the blue waters of Llyn Ogwen at its foot, is the well-loved Milestone Buttress, which leads the eye up the north ridge of Tryfan to its summit.

Bridges ancient and modern

Under the arch of the modern road-bridge by
Ogwen Falls lies an older one, possibly built by
the Romans.

Y Garn

This mountain rises to the west of Cwm Idwal
and may be ascended direct. You can also climb
it by a more circuitous route via the path to the
left of the Devil's Kitchen, bearing right when
you reach the plateau above.

Three llynnau

(overleaf)

From the summit of Y Garn, three llynnau are seen below: Clyd, Idwal and Ogwen. They all lie at different levels. This viewpoint may be reached from Cwm Idwal.

The Glyders from Y Garn

This picture encompasses, from the left, Glyder
Fach, the Castle of the Winds, and Glyder Fawr.
Llyn y Cwn is just visible on the right.

Llyn Idwal

What could be more restful than this shimmering
lake on a lovely day, with Pen yr Ole Wen
reflected on its surface?

Cwm Idwal

(overleaf)

This fine photograph of the cirque of cliffs at the head of the cwm clearly shows the cleft of Twll Du (the Devil's Kitchen) in the centre. The walker who wishes to attain the plateau above should take the path that leads up on the left.

Llyn Bochlwyd

(overleaf pp 64/65)

The Gribin Ridge and Y Garn, lightly veiled in cloud, loom over this lake whose shape is reminiscent of the outline of Australia. It is passed during a walk from Ogwen Cottage to Bwlch Tryfan.

Bristly Ridge

This savage-looking northern spur of Glyder Fach may be used as a scrambling route to the summit. It is seen here beautifully mirrored in Llyn Caseg ffraith.

Afon Dudodyn

This enchanting stream rises under Elidir Fawr
and ripples down to Nant Peris. If you are
climbing Elidir Fawr by this route, it is at the
bridge seen here that the steep part commences.

Elidir Fawr and Marchlyn Mawr

This tranquil scene gives no clue to the activities
hidden underground! Marchlyn Mawr is now
part of the Dinorwic pump storage scheme: it is
the upper reservoir whose waters flow through
turbines concealed in the mountain to Llyn Peris
below.

Marchlyn Bach
(overleaf)

This sapphire lake lies a little below its larger sister: it is seen here with one ridge of Elidir Fach descending on the left, and a view of the coast in the far distance.

Snowdon from the Capel Pinnacles
(overleaf pp 74/75)

Morning light touches this beautiful scene with gold. From this viewpoint the eye passes over the Llynnau Mymbyr and along Nant y gwryd, to the stupendous grandeur of the Snowdon Horseshoe on the horizon.

Snowdon from Llynnau Mymbyr
(overleaf pp 76/77)

Part of the Snowdon group is here seen reflected in the more westerly of the two lakes which lie beside the road from Capel Curig to Pen y Gwryd.

Llanberis Pass from Clogwyn Station

From Clogwyn Station on the Snowdon Railway,
Glyder Fawr, with its outcrop Esgair Felen, is
seen across the deep trench that carries the
Llanberis Pass. This rises to Pen y Pass on the
right, with Moel Siabod seen on the skyline
beyond.

The Pyg track

This popular track, after leaving Pen y Pass, meanders over Bwlch y Moch and along the flanks of both Crib Goch and Crib y Ddysgl, with views of Llyn Llydaw below. It finally reaches Bwlch Glas, where it joins the Llanberis path to the summit of Snowdon.

Llyn Teyrn

This delectable tarn is passed when ascending the
Miner's Track, before reaching the shore of Llyn
Llydaw. In this superb picture the outline of
Lliwedd is mirrored in the tarn's limpid surface.

Snowdon and Crib Goch

(overleaf)

Viewed from the Miner's Track the eastern ridge of Crib Goch is very clearly seen on the right, with Snowdon to the left.

Snowdon from Llyn Llydaw

(overleaf pp 86/87)

The majestic bulk of Yr Wyddfa is seen here with a light dusting of snow. This viewpoint is one of the most popular for a study of Wales's highest mountain.

Crib Goch from Llyn Llydaw

Seen across the lake this grand mountain assumes
a quite different shape. On the right, the east ridge
leads to the summit.

Glaslyn and Llyn Llydaw

Once you reach the zig-zags below Bwlch Glas,
as you climb towards the summit of Snowdon,
these two lakes can be seen far below, as you look
back.

Almost there

The Snowdon Railway runs between Llanberis
and the summit of Yr Wyddfa. Here the
passengers are nearly at the end of their exciting
journey, with a magnificent panorama to the west.

Crib y Ddysgl

(overleaf)

If the Snowdon Horseshoe is walked in an anti-clockwise direction Crib y Ddysgl is traversed after Crib Goch. It is seen here from the summit of Snowdon.

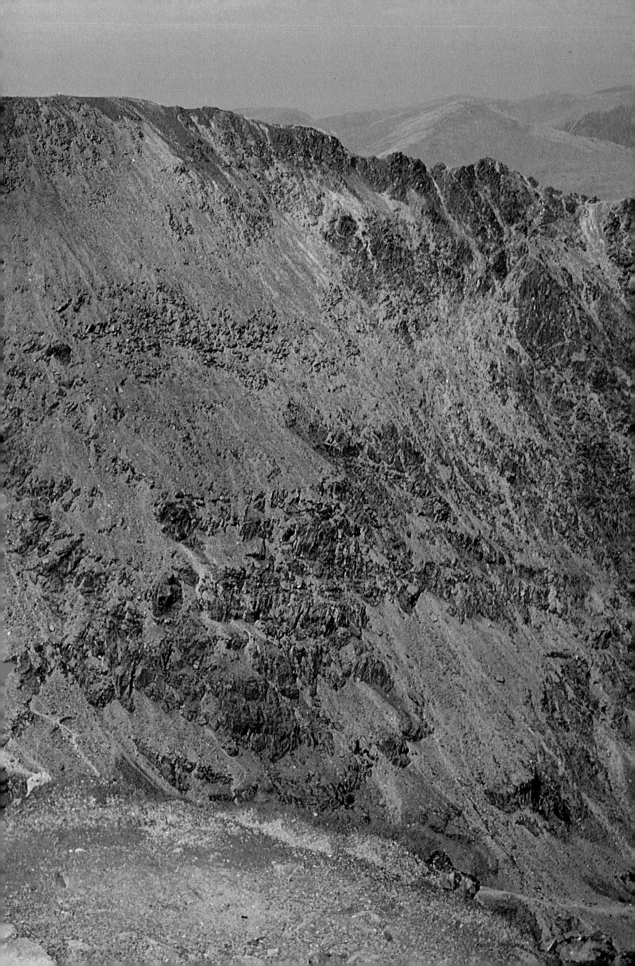

Lliwedd from Bwlch y Moch

From this viewpoint, looking across and beyond
Llyn Llydaw, the soaring cliffs of Lliwedd are the
most prominent feature. Bwlch y Saethau appears
on the right.

Crib Goch

Viewed here from Crib y Ddysgl in evening light,
the sheer precipices of this side of the mountain
are clearly evident. To the right the path is seen
descending from the Pinnacles towards Bwlch
Coch.

99

Llyn Glas

An indistinct path leaves the Pyg track near a
derelict sheepfold and leads to diminutive Llyn
Glas, which nestles below Clogwyn y Person. The
area is renowned for its alpine flora.

The Glyders from Llyn Glas
(overleaf)

From this lovely little tarn a fine view of the southern elevation of the Glyders is revealed beyond the Llanberis Pass.

The Glyders from The Gwynant valley
(overleaf pp 104/105)

From the Gwynant valley, however, a quite different view of this fine group of mountains may be enjoyed.

Llyn Gwynant

The road from Pen y Gwryd to Beddgelert
descends towards the Gwynant valley, and where
it levels out you come upon this lovely lake.

In the Gwynant valley

The Afon Glaslyn meanders down the Gwynant
valley, passing through both Llyn Gwynant and
Llyn Dinas before reaching Beddgelert.

Yr Aran from Llyn Gwynant
(*overleaf*)

The rippling waters of Llyn Gwynant afford a beautiful foreground for Yr Aran, here seen mantled with early snow.

The Watkin Path
(*overleaf pp 112/113*)

This popular path to Snowdon leaves Nant Gwynant near Pont Bethania and passes through Cwm y llan to reach Bwlch y Saethau, where it turns left for the summit.

Afon Cwmllan Waterfall

The cascades of this charming waterfall are seen on the right of the Watkin Path just before entering Cwm y llan.

Gladstone Rock

Situated beside the Watkin Path in Cwm y llan,
this tablet commemorates the opening of the path
by Mr Gladstone in 1892 when he was 83.

Yr Aran

A track leaving the Watkin Path near Plas Cwm
llan leads to the summit of this peak, which is seen
here from the west, rearing its head against the
clouds.

Snowdon from the Rhyd-ddu path
(*overleaf*)

The path from Rhyd-ddu is a very popular route up Snowdon. It passes along the summit ridge of Llechog (seen here with Snowdon beyond it) and ascends the Saddle by an eroded track, before finally reaching the summit over Bwlch Main.

Cwm Clogwyn from Llechog
(*overleaf pp 122/123*)

Cwm Clogwyn, cradled by the ridges of Clogwyn D'ur Arddu to the north and Llechog to the south, bites deeply into the bulk of Snowdon. As the map shows, it encompasses five small sheets of water, only three of which are named.

Clogwyn Du'r Arddu

The crest of this magnificent cliff, which is so well
known to climbers, lies close to the Snowdon
Ranger path. Carnedd Ugain is seen in the
distance, with a train crossing its flank on the way
to the Snowdon summit station.

Moel Siabod

(overleaf)

If you are approaching Snowdonia from the east, this shapely peak, which rises above Capel Curig, is the first you will see and is a fine introduction to the area. It is photographed here from the north-east, reflected in the still waters of the Afon Llugwy.

Old quarry workings

During the ascent of Moel Siabod by the track
that starts near Pont Cyfyng, and before reaching
Llyn y Foel, you will pass through an old quarry
where this deep pool lies beside the path. As it is
unfenced, it is prudent to be careful here.

The Dolwyddelan Ridge

This ridge is a prominent feature of Moel Siabod when viewed from the shore of Llyn y Foel. A good path on the ridge leads to the summit.

Looking north from Moel Siabod

(overleaf)

The descending north ridge of the peak is pictured here from the Dolwyddelan Ridge, with a wonderful view towards the north coast of Wales beyond it. Llyn y Foel is out of sight below, to the right.

Descending the track

(overleaf pp 134/135)

Below the quarry workings which were passed on the ascent of Moel Siabod lies this lonely and un-named sheet of water. It was once a reservoir for quarries, long abandoned, lower down.

Llyn Llagi

Llyn Llagi is one of the so-called 'Dog Lakes' and
may be reached by a track leaving the side road
which runs from Nant Gwynant to the villge of
Nantmor.

Cnicht

(overleaf)

This shapely peak, seen here to advantage from the south, lies at the southern end of the Moel Siabod group of hills, and may easily be ascended from Croesor.

Cnicht from near Tan Lan

(overleaf pp 140/141)

The road bridge over the Afon Croesor on the A487 provides an excellent foreground for this closer shot of the splendid peak. I have heard Cnicht referred to as 'The Welsh Matterhorn'.

The summit ridge of Cnicht

The summit ridge of this mountain yields a grand
panorama: looking south, you can see the shining
waters of Tremadoc Bay in the distance.

Llyn Cwmorthin
(*overleaf*)

This quiet valley containing many quarry workings may be reached easily from Tanygrisiau, or from the other side by a longer walk up Cwm Croesor and over Bwlch Rhosydd.

Cnicht and the Moelwyns
(*overleaf pp 146/147*)

The Moelwyns, Mawr and Bach, lie to the east of Cnicht, and are separated from it by the delightful and lonely Cwm Croesor.

The Moelwyns from the south

The bulk of Moelwyn Mawr, on the left, is joined
to that of Moelwyn Bach by Craig Ysgafn. The
heights may be gained via a path leading from the
road that runs between Croesor and Rhyd.

Llyn Stwlan

This forms the upper reservoir for the power
station at Tanygrisiau, and it lies beneath the
crags of Craig Ysgafn.

Port Meirion

This romantic Italianate village, part of which is seen here, was created by the late Sir Clough Williams-Ellis beside the waters of Traeth Bach, near Porthmadog.

The river in Beddgelert

(overleaf)

In this charming village where three valleys meet, the Afon Colwyn rushes into the Afon Glaslyn, which then turns south, eventually reaching the sea at Porthmadog.

Gelert's grave

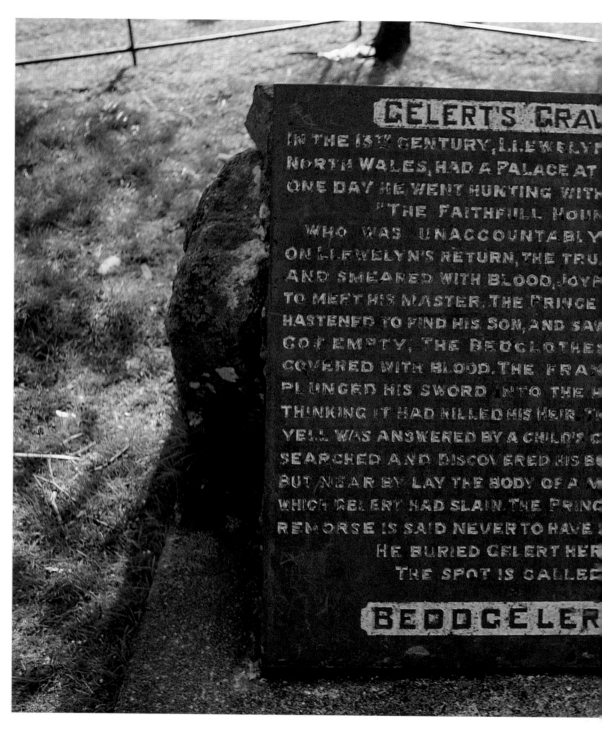

Those visiting Beddgelert will probably have heard the legend of Gelert, the faithful hound. This tablet marks the supposed site of his last resting-place.

Old tunnels at Beddgelert

A railway once went northwards from
Porthmadog through Beddgelert: this was where
the track ran, south of the village. Its traverse
makes an interesting and entertaining ramble
above the Afon Glaslyn.

Llyn Dinas

This charming lake, perfectly captured as it
sparkles in the summer sun, lies beside the road
to the north-east of Beddgelert. A fine view of
Moel Hebog may be obtained from its outflow.

Moel Hebog and its satellites

(overleaf)

From Moel Hebog on the left the ridge runs over Moel yr Ogof and terminates with Moel Lefn. This group lies to the west of Beddgelert.

Moel Hebog in cloud

(overleaf pp 164/165)

This unusual picture was taken from Lliwedd, on a day when the cloud was down in the valleys. The summit of Yr Aran can be seen, making a foreground to Moel Hebog.

Y Garn II *from Llyn y Gadair*

Y Garn (qualified by the Roman II to distinguish
it from its namesake in the Glyders group) lies at
the north-eastern end of the Nantlle Ridge.
Mynydd Mawr is seen on the skyline to the right.

Mynydd Drws-y-coed

If walking the Nantlle Ridge in a south-westerly direction, the sharp prow of this peak is the first you will encounter after Y Garn. It is followed by Trum-y-Ddysgl and Mynydd Talmignedd, before you reach Craig Cwmsilyn.

Cwm Silyn

As you approach the ridge from the west, the
great slab of Cwm Silyn catches the light high on
the right. The lake below it is one of the Llynnau
Cwmsilyn.

The Nantlle Ridge

On reaching Craig Cwmsilyn you will be amply
rewarded by the view back over this lovely ridge,
which reveals Snowdon in all its majesty in the
distance.

Mynydd Mawr from Y Garn II
(overleaf)

This mountain, lying to the north-west of the Nantlle Ridge across the pass of Drws-y-coed, is fronted by the shattered crags of Craig y Bera.

Snowdon from Mynydd Mawr

The imposing outline of Snowdon is seen here
beyond Nant y Betws, with the head of Llyn
Cwellyn below.

Craig y Bera

The bare, riven pinnacles of Craig y Bera consist
of rock which has been eroded by the elements,
and should be avoided. A path from Planydd farm
near Llyn Cwellyn passes to the right of them on
the way to the summit of Mynydd Mawr.

Snowdon from Drws-y-coed pass

(*overleaf*)

This pass connects Rhyd-ddu and the village of Nantlle. It is well worth stopping here to enjoy the superb prospect of Snowdon.

The Moel Eilio ridge from Moel yr Ogof

(*overleaf pp 182/183*)

Moel Eilio stands at the western end of the ridge that descends from Snowdon over the crest of Clogwyn D'ur Arddu to Bwlch cwm-brwynog, before passing over Moel Cynghorion and Foel-goch.

Llyn Cwellyn

This much-loved lake lies beside the road from
Beddgelert to Caernarfon. The Snowdon Ranger
Youth Hostel is on the other side of the road and
it is here that the path of the same name begins
its ascent of Snowdon.

Caernarfon Castle

This splendidly restored thirteenth-century castle was the birthplace of Edward II, the first Prince of Wales. Prince Charles was here presented to the people of Wales in 1969.

Snowdon from Llyn Padarn

(overleaf)

The Snowdon group, bathed in evening light, makes a perfect backdrop for the still waters of Llyn Padarn, which lies to the west of Llanberis.

Llyn Celyn and Arennig Fawr

(overleaf pp 190/191)

Llyn Celyn is a reservoir passed when you take the road from Ffestiniog to Bala. From its shore there is this memorable view of the north-west aspect of Arennig Fawr.

Arennig Fawr from its Llyn

The Arennig group of hills lies amid barren moorland between Ffestiniog and Bala Lake. This peak is the highest of the group, and beneath its frowning cliffs lies Llyn Arennig Fawr, to the east.

The Arans from Bala Lake

(overleaf)

The Aran group, seen on the far horizon beneath a magnificent cloudscape, contains the highest ridge in Wales south of the Snowdon area.

Harlech Castle

(overleaf pp 196/197)

The town of Harlech on Tremadoc Bay boasts this fine thirteenth-century castle. From its walls the prospect to the distant north reveals this view of Snowdon.

The Rhinogs from the east

An idyllic Welsh country scene. This group of mountains is part of a long backbone of hills overlooking Tremadoc Bay and known collectively as 'The Harlech Dome'. From the left the peaks are Y Llethr, Rhinog Fach and Rhinog Fawr.

The path to Cwm y Cau
(*overleaf*)

Moving south beyond Barmouth, you will encounter the grandeur of the Cadair Idris massif. The mountain may be climbed by a path from near Tal-y-llyn which threads this cwm on the way.

Pen y Gadair

This is the dominant peak in the Cadair Idris
group: it is seen here from Craig y Cau.

Cyfrwy and Barmouth from Pen y Gadair

(overleaf)

There is a spectacular view from Pen y Gadair – the cliffs of Cyfrwy are backed by the grassy western ridge of Cadair Idris, with Barmouth and its railway bridge spanning the estuary of the Afon Mawddach far to the right.

Tal-y-llyn

This beautiful lake, renowned for its fishing, lies
on the road from Dolgellau to Towyn.
Accommodation can be found here by those
wishing to explore Cadair Idris.

The Bird Rock
(overleaf)

Also known as Craig yr Aderyn, this is aptly
named as it is the haunt of birds of many species.
It overlooks the valley of Dysynni to the north-
east of Towyn.

Aberdovey
(overleaf pp 210/211)

This charming resort, with extensive sands, lies at
the mouth of the River Dovey on Cardigan Bay.
It is just inside the boundary of the Snowdonia
National Park, and here we end our journey
through this beautiful region of Wales.